STRAY

African
POETRY
BOOK SERIES

Series editor: Kwame Dawes

STRAY

Bernard Farai Matambo

Foreword by Kwame Dawes

University of Nebraska Press
Lincoln and London

Acknowledgments for the use of copyrighted
material appear on pages 75–76, which
constitute an extension of the copyright page.

The African Poetry Book Series has been made
possible through the generosity of philanthropists
Laura and Robert F. X. Sillerman, whose
contributions have facilitated the establishment
and operation of the African Poetry Book Fund.

Library of Congress Cataloging-in-Publication Data
Names: Matambo, Bernard Farai, author. | Dawes,
Kwame Senu Neville, 1962– writer of foreword.
Title: Stray / Bernard Farai Matambo;
foreword by Kwame Dawes.
Description: Lincoln: University of Nebraska
Press, [2018] | Series: African poetry book series
Identifiers: LCCN 2017043648
ISBN 9781496205582 (hardcover: acid-free paper)
ISBN 9781496207791 (epub)
ISBN 9781496207807 (mobi)
ISBN 9781496207814 (pdf)
Classification: LCC PS3613.A822 A6 2018
| DDC 811/.6—dc23 LC record available
at https://lccn.loc.gov/2017043648

Set in Garamond Premier by Mikala R Kolander.

CONTENTS

FOREWORD

Kwame Dawes

Bernard Matambo's *Stray* joins an illustrious group of debut collections in this series. Matambo's penchant for the prose-shaped line, and his persistent sense that contradictory impulses in poetry are necessary for a poet in search of emotional and intellectual truth, shine throughout this moving collection of poems. Yet what remains as the hallmark of these poems is their reach for images that reflect invention and precision: "The mountains were full of song, their trembling not our enemy" ("All the Merry Hills").

Matambo takes us through several key familial (father, brother, and mother) relationships that have symbolic value, as each allows him to explore broader issues of identity, place, and ideology in intellectually complex ways. In poems that explore the legacy of a masculine indiscretion and cruelty, there is a clear sense that the son is seen as an inheritor of sins from the father. Rather than blame, the speaker appears to be caught in an inevitability, a twisted notion of a birthright. And in this, there is in the beauty of the language, the invention of description, a quality of empathy caught in the memory of a father who whimpers after orgasm with his long-suffering wife, a man at once flawed and, thus, human:

It was a sport I knew little of then
except for the beads in the corners of his eyes
when he returned delicate with his thunders.
    ("In the Name of the Tongue")

The father, though, will fail, and the mother will leave. The father, caught in both regret and a strange kind of unhinged hope, waits for her return, expecting it, even as he holds onto the one thing he has left: the totems of his tribe. Again and again, Matambo offsets a penchant for acrimony and blame by turning these poems of censure into poems of quiet confession: "Sometimes I catch him in the taste of my tongue" ("In the Name of the Father").

In the opening poems, Matambo variously describes the legacy of the speaker's father as a stain, an inheritance, a taste, and a residual sense of self; and much of what gives these poems tension is their attempt to outline what is clearly religious hypocrisy with the necessity for respect—if not love. These poems move through narrative "confessions" on behalf of the father into a reluctant sense of complicity: "It all begins with the stain of him, the marrow / leaking out into the bone" ("Holy Ghost").

The stain returns around matters of faith and desire. And in this, Matambo writes as a poet excavating themes that haunt the young writer—the discovery of desire, the disquiet and excitement of troubled faith, and the hunger to find language to express all of this. He is both ironic and sincere in the belief that poetry cannot contain these feelings:

Remind me again, dear love, of that time when the world was as young as we were and I was lit bright with urges, light as the shroud Christ yielded when he gave up his tomb, sick of sleeping alone and dreading the eternity of it, when he sought himself some company. Of this no poetry shall come.
    ("Catechism")

The father functions as an intellectual trigger for the poet such that even as he contemplates, in the brilliantly realized long poem that explores the story of Ota Benga ("Ota Benga Returns to the Congo"), it is the father who Matambo connects with Benga before making his own symbolic connection to the complex figure. Ota Benga, of course, is the Congolese man who at the turn of the last century was made a spectacle of in the United States as a zoo dweller:

> I remember nothing of what riled the orangutan
> inside the cage deep inside my father, the one
> he concealed so long and deep in him like a bad habit
> until it too raged for its freedom, and my father placed his pistol
> on De Boer's ear. I too sometimes hear its rolling call in my bones.

From that connection created by a drunk father's witty reflection, "Was Ota Benga the first Afropolitan—" we arrive at the "call in my bones" of Matambo, whose task is to find a thread of connection even as he is coming into his own—straying, as it were from home. But what remains strikingly inventive and impressive about Matambo is the complex thinking that allows him in this poem to offer a very contemporary examination of the persistent relationship between the West and Africa and how it is played out in the intimate place of the psyche. Ota Benga, Saartjie Baartman, Matambo's father (whose narrative includes an act of violence that is heightened by the willful treatment of it as something that could be more than symbolic), and Matambo himself are deeply connected—they are wrestling with the idea of being viewed as subhuman spectacles by white culture and with the implications of return to the "motherland" once the knowledge of what is out there has corrupted them.

XIX

> Before the credits climb up the screen
> closing the film on his life, Ota Benga
> in the stadium at Matadi rises from his seat
> and surveys the floodlights undressing
> the audience aching for him to speak.

Dear Gentlemen of the Academy: I wish
I was not the music the bow offers the mouth
the arrow leaps out to touch
saying, I am a man, I am a man, I am a man!

The poem serves as a fit segue into poems that reflect Matambo's exploration of the complications of the immigrant's life in America. In poems like "You Don't Want the Light to Find Out What You've Done," much of this is reduced to a peculiar but seemingly necessary excavation of race in America: "I am still wondering about being black enough." The African man traveling through Nebraska with a woman who could pass as Persian "when the weather permits" throws out the clichés of race, MLK, collard greens, Mike Tyson, lynching, and ends with a vulnerability that is admirable and troubling:

I am in want of my egg over easy, my sunny-side up. I am still searching for a room dark enough to hang my skin in, let the light come in.

But it is exactly this kind of "uncomfortable" articulation—these confessions that amount to questions that unsettle the idea of race that makes Matambo wholly modern and necessary for these times. He is fully aware of the artifice of art, the ways in which language shapes sentiment and the way meaning can be manipulated by the poem. That self-awareness proves refreshing because it comes to us as a genuinely sincere willingness to press for truth. In "Diallo" his identification with the young African immigrant killed by police in New York is subject to scrutiny:

Here is a scene, Diallo studying by night, his stoic hopes
in a mound beside him, noosed by the chains that sunk
the names of his ancestors in the crossing. Because I am
sentimental he will study by candlelight. Because reason

will prevail, he will study the wisdom of the crow.
This of course is a lie.

Matambo builds his mythology of exile and return that will echo through this collection, where return is a constantly troubled notion marked by the years of ideological dismantling and rebuilding around issues of negritude, Pan Africanism, and Afropolitanism, all of which are contained in the figures of both Diallo and also Cato, a kind of alter ego who is full of dreams of return. Images of the disquiet of postcolonial Africa is explored through figures like Lumumba, who is forgiven for his idealism because he "did not know [at the time of his execution] the [Pan Africanist] tree was corrupt." These poems are full of a longing for meaning and value, a longing that, in this case, highlights absence and need, which is not there and thus can be read through the archaism of that which is "wanting."

I want so much to believe in the goodness of the ape within me,
he said, the highway behind us roaring with the weight
of our American dream.

The worlds that Matambo creates have the uncanny ability to be fully rooted in the details of an earthly existence marked by the specifics of survival in "independent" Zimbabwe—the riots, the dying currency, the challenges of finding food—and yet are filled with the strange mystery of the surreal, the inexplicable, the confoundingly spiritual:

That year it rained crows. Birds fell out of the sky in midflight. Their squawking made mother nervous. It gave her the chills and made her teeth chatter. She threw her eyes everywhere, and through the window caught the taut sky tightening.
("Feasts for the Blind")

The swelling dead crows will soon become the bodies of corpses floating down a river, and the worlds that Matambo creates in the third movement of the collection build an extensive prose narrative broken up into small chapters that reflect on the memory of home, a home that is presumably in the "ghettos" of Harare, in which the mother is the protagonist—the one who sees all, the one whose story is told. It is a story that has the quality of fable, a cautionary tale about the many revolutions that have marked the continent as a whole. Matambo's vision for these revolutions is not positive. The narrative is the same. Long-suffering people wait and wait until their suffering becomes too much, and so they rise up, and they revolt, and they eventually "triumph" only long enough to see that what they have won is another epoch of suffering. One could accuse Matambo of cynicism in passages like this:

> We trudged about and salvaged the remains of past civilizations. Stretches of asphalt that betrayed old roads. Shards of cheap crockery and half-burnt books, dolls with singed hair. Fat men loitered in abandoned alleyways. They clasped their offspring to their chests like secrets. They cast telling eyes on us. Out in the distance, the begging cup still clanged.
> ("The City")

But *Stray* manages to test this cynicism in its tender and unsettled exploration of the self. And here again we see that one of the complicated features of longing and need is the implicit understanding that there exists in the body a capacity to be satisfied. The sequence of poems "Requiem: In the Case Regarding My Brother" represents exactly that elegant and moving combining of loss and necessary hope in art:

> Because belief too is an act of faith, I believed the wound in my brother would liberate him to the music within him.
> ("viii")

> The hunger within him worried me with song.
> ("xiv")

These contradictory omens are the hallmark of this collection, and it is in their emotional uncertainty that we recognize the inevitability of poetry that has the capacity to unsettle the dangers of assurance

It is impossible to come from stretches of verse like this without having a sense that the poet has sought to contain in this hymn to his brother, who is at once to himself and to the artist who must work within the limitations and possibilities of being part of the "skinfolk":

> My brother said something was tightening within him. He was looking, he said, for more space to move within his skin.
>
> I worried with understanding. It was a hunger I knew could not be diminished. Colossal in its cravings, unimpeachable with its facts.
>
> The sculpture he was building fashioned a cage around him. On its roof, drawn out bales of cotton, a thicket of nooses dangling like neckties.
>
> The leg irons, he said, were the only symbolism.
> ("vii")

The two poems that end the collection return us to the challenges of exile and loss and the combination of belonging and un-belonging that marks and fascinates Matambo. In the third part of "Mugarandega," "Akanga nyimo avangarara" ("Them who have chosen to roast round nuts must stay the course"), an anecdote unfolds with characteristic mysteriousness and significance. The "you," one imagines, is the lyric "I":

> Once, in a foreign land, you muttered confusedly, *Breath is a syllable cremation cannot afford*, then alighted the train to hug the first African you saw, because they were African. The scent of his sweat, raw shea butter, sage, and cinnamon. His glow carried you back up the mountains. Flame lilies and lavender; aloe and rose. Still after all you

wish to be buried among your kin. You fear the weight of return the way you fear in death the earth pressing down against your corpse will snap your clavicle into two.

And in "In the Throat of the Heaven's Guide," we find a work of deep and dark wit that comes as close as Matambo will get to addressing the dictatorship that has ruled Zimbabwe for decades. Here, however, the names mentioned and the figures alluded to are part of the rogue gallery of dictators including Idi Amin, Saddam Hussein, Mobutu Sese Seko, and Sani Abacha. The leader's reported struggles with prostate cancer and his peculiar predilection are given only veiled treatment here, and yet what comes of this musing on the illness that dictators face is a cryptic statement that leaves us with a puzzle to solve: "Born of the gun. Give me sight, so I too may see. An eye for an eye, our scrambled world."

STRAY

Preamble to Stray

We forgot the unsubtle pleasures of the light. And because we forgot the pleasures of the light, we forgot what beauty resided in the shadows, what we possessed. The city lay within us, dark, dank, and skeletal. We forgot the rooted scent of our dreams. And because we forgot the rooted scent of our dreams, we forgot they could flower. No, not anymore; no longer could everyone read the coming air for the rain. Everything knew its way around everything else, you said. Quietly I nursed my doubts. We lost the petals of the flowers within us; we forgot the radiance of their color. And because we forgot the radiance of their color, we wandered about the city and worried its ruins with our suffering. The city lay within us, dark, dank, and hungry.

All the Merry Hills

Say there is another story we will not share here, let us assume this to be true.

Say at a later time, there is a *We* to be engaged, one in which you and I fit in that tight a space with minimal panic.

You could say something about the weather and I could make a remark on how pleasant the bells peel every other hour flooding the trees with their trembling.

Say you could be still upon noticing you were becoming undone, as though you were the bridal lace on the big day. You are neither the bride nor the groom, but you are up there with the cool of them. Say you were one of the multitudes around us: you, too, rooted in the wealth of your pronouncements.

Once, in the dark, I mistook a hanging hose for a broken noose. In the silence of all that is good between us, I could not provoke inquiries. The mountains were full of song, their trembling not our enemy.

In the Name of the Tongue

Come Sunday afternoon and I sat back hunched
in the car, thumbing my father's Bible, the door slamming

behind him, as though his gun had burst a nest of birds.
I fingered the grime farther into my hair and sat rehearsing,

Thou shalt not steal, Thou shalt not bear false witness,
Thou shalt not covet thy neighbor's house,

my father's sweet-tongued weights turning coolly on my tongue
as I thought again of that verse where the woman

wets Jesus' feet with her tears and mops them away with her hair,
the lean, long day sliding past, hot in the nest of my jaw.

It was always the same house we stopped at, Baba and I,
the one whose eaves hung low like the milkman's sly eyes

when they followed Patience Wida's behind
and made him clang his bell more slowly.

How afterward Mami's anger rose when she caught
the jasmine and talc tight on his neck

like a noose. Something must have burst holy out of her
those nights, all night her tongue flailing,

fire coming down through the walls louder
than when they made love, and he whimpered afterward.

How I reached into the darkness and tongued
the contours of his sins.

Thou shalt not steal, Thou shalt not bear false witness,
Thou shalt not covet thy neighbor's house.

It was a sport I knew little of then
except for the beads in the corners of his eyes

when he returned delicate with his thunders.
He liked golf best, and always took me to the driving range

afterward, his hand in a glove, holding firm his stick.
Tomorrow, he said, you will learn how to drive.

In the Name of the Father

after Espada

My father sat in the back pew nursing his doubts.
All he had left was his totem. The names of his clan

turned on his tongue until the incense died down.
Afterward he walked for hours in the dark

fine-tuning his hearing aid, hoping to hear God.
He exceled in the dark like a root.

The glow that shed off him tangled good women,
sweet music, and tar.

The night she left him he said, The dead
have no shadows, then waited for his luck to turn

in the keyhole the way the heart
turns slovenly with remorse.

At night he slung her dress across his thigh
and mended the holes in the armpits.

He turned the names of his fears over and over
in his mouth, like a morsel of meat one chews for the salt

but won't swallow until the tongue scars.

Wars, he said, have been ended this way; you stitch
your way right across the stains.

The year he learned to type, he crouched in the dust
and sketched with his fingers the house

he would build when she came back to him begging.
The words he practiced made his mouth twitch.

Sometimes I catch him in the taste of my tongue.

Holy Ghost

It all begins with the stain of him, the marrow
leaking out into the bone. We are driving through the dark

without headlights when Norma mentions the ghost
I have all along nursed in my blood, how only after forgetting

her Bible in her preacher father's car did she find the girl in whose
jawline and slow eyes her father too resided. He must

have slipped the photo of the girl in the book
of Exodus while preparing a sermon on idolatry,

the dull-eyed girl lanky beside him in the picture,
astute in her Catholic school uniform

and every bit the maid Norma's mother had fired years ago
for more than missing laundry. We drove for hours

in silence afterward through the rain,
the hailstorm beating alive within me,

Confess, confess, confess. How I could have wept
the tears arresting my burdened tongue.

Catechism

April 1994

You must have known better. Twelve years old and you were in the perfect blur of the world, the nuns like fire ants crawling everywhere, worried sick out of their habits and pantyhose. Particularly Sister Bettina.

Sister Bettina and her breasts, the daft youth in her knowing eye, and how the catechism class numbers kept climbing up over them, as though they were the very fountain of youth lit with the very song from the Pied Piper of Hamelin's wet dream, the one in which the children return to him, their nimble mothers in tow.

Because who didn't want to be saved by her, be confirmed in the flesh of her low hips, learn how to receive the body of Christ with a throbbing jaw, an anarchy of gears shifting between your adolescent thighs as her lower lip curled, pleading for the mercy of her open tongue saying, The Body of Christ; the Body of Christ, Amen.

Because that must have been when I saw the light of my bearings and yet was left longing for it to cut me through to blindness. My eyes shied away, the quiet limbs on the convent's screen washing in the foam of the stream. The thwarted hack of an axe through brawn, a brow wet with the effort of it. And then they were coming, bodies tumbling down the stream like manna from heaven.

Remind me again, dear love, of that time when the world was as young as we were and I was lit bright with urges, light as the shroud Christ yielded when he gave up his tomb, sick of sleeping alone and dreading the eternity of it, when he sought himself some company. Of this no poetry shall come.

Ota Benga Returns to the Congo

I

Once, after he was drunk, my father blurted out,
Was Ota Benga the first Afropolitan—
Negritude encountered after its own hangover?
then leaned into his sleep soon as C parted his lips,
the storm clouds quietening within him like an orangutan's.

II

All the way we go. The night we dig up Ota Benga's remains
we are neck deep in the muck, heads above ground
on grass. Our fingers, C said, carried most silence in the dark.
I believed no word of it. The grave smelled most of wood smoke and funk,
the piranhas in Benga's mouth pearl white and everywhere.

III

Here is what the paper said of him that September:
Good head, bright eyes, a pleasing countenance.
He is not hairy, is not covered by the downy fell
described by some explorers. Happiest when at work.

IV

I remember nothing of what riled the orangutan
inside the cage deep inside my father, the one
he concealed so long and deep in him like a bad habit
until it too raged for its freedom, and my father placed his pistol
on De Boer's ear. I too sometimes hear its rolling call in my bones.

V

Said the reverend once again alive

with frustration: Our race, we think,
is depressed enough without exhibiting
one of us with the apes.

VI

The secretary of the zoo at the time
was a eugenicist, Madison Grant. His writings
on the dangers of inferior races outbreeding
and mixed breeding with Caucasians
earned him bowed heads and Europraises.

VII

Look, I said, I know nothing about this, not anymore
than you do. I too wish I could dance myself free.
I have the feeling I've lived in the empire of the zoo
before. I too have shouldered a fondness for orangutans.

VIII

Dear Bingo. I am not the music the arrow leaves behind
with the bow when it leaps off to find flesh on its own.
Once sober, my father said, If you stare long enough
at the horizon you will catch the last slave ship ploughing
its way back to Africa with our kin. I screwed my eyes
on the horizon until they burned with the blood.

IX

I wanted to touch the joy my father carried with him
after the police had accepted his bribe for driving
under the influence. In the backseat on the highway
back to The Motherland, Ota Benga assembles himself
bone against bone, eyes blind and eager like a newborn's.
Only then do I see everything said about the horizon is true.

X

Once in the dark I awoke on a fresh grave
in the middle of a cane field, the fur in my mouth
wet with blood. Aching for insight, I chipped
and chipped at my teeth until my blood filled with song.
Aching for insight, I chipped and chipped at my teeth
but the gunshot sound would not leave me.

XI

That afternoon the clouds swirled inside my father.
Half man, half anger, the no-man's-land in him
proclaimed away from the middle ground and announced
the missing link in the zoo. I chipped and chipped at my teeth
until my blood filled with song.

XII

One with a tongue armed with the armor
of obvious things says in the newspaper: We send
our missionaries to Africa to Christianize them
then we bring one here to brutalize him.

XIII

My report will not teach the Academy anything basically new.
The first thing I learned was to shake hands, I will say.
Every wanderer on earth feels a little tickling in his heels.
Every wanderer on earth feels a little tickling in his heels.

XIV

After the reverend is once again alive
with frustration, he announces, We are frank
enough to say we don't like this exhibition
of one of our own race with monkeys.

XV

Miles afterward C startles awake, the world still young
as him whizzing past his window. The dream
in his eyes still carries flowers of his goodness. We are
miles away still from the Motherland, but already
the horizon is alive with the wagging tongues of ceremonial fires.

XVI

I never carried an orangutan as big as the one
my father kept barricaded deep inside him
behind the parting in his hair and good diction
searching for a way out. Avoidance of all willfulness
was the supreme commandment he imposed on himself,
until he heard the gunshot leap from his hand.

XVII

O where are you Saartjie Baartman
you whose roots leaked the seed of their blood
into me. I want to worship before the altar
of your symbolism, the altar whose behind
White men stained with longing.

XVIII

Afterward, I lifted my hands and took no pleasure
in lifting the sky. After everything had freed him,
my father still believed geography of origin remained
our indictment. For years I too would not heed his call.
I chipped at my teeth but my blood would not fill with song.

XIX

Before the credits climb up the screen
closing the film on his life, Ota Benga

in the stadium at Matadi rises from his seat
and surveys the floodlights undressing
the audience aching for him to speak.

xx

Dear Gentlemen of the Academy: I wish
I was not the music the bow offers the mouth
the arrow leaps out to touch
saying, I am a man, I am a man, I am a man!

You Don't Want the Light to Find
Out What You've Done

You, me, and Martin Luther King Jr. being black together. We are on a highway, somewhere where the corn is low, holding its ears in. As if the Indian bones in these hills had something to say. You tell me it's Nebraska. That corn looks Nebraskan is your excuse. The way my girl could be Persian when the weather permits.

We have given speeches for free before, but not since Iowa. Iowa has been our dessert. We are off now west on the gravy train, our lungs beating virginal across the open states. Where did they lynch men like me for gazing too long at white women?

Everywhere. In Illinois they hung two men near the Blue Front. And not until 1942 was a man tried for holding another man captive. For labor. That was the nearly true end of slavery. But still I am waiting for a morsel of good faith at the courts of public opinion on the redemption of Iron Mike Tyson. Waiting for my fist to clear the foggy eye of God. The way VD shots calm down the particulars, keep the herpes away, watching by the rubble.

And I too used to think these tollgates here were border posts up in arms, uniting the states. And this country here was one huge jukebox. It explained the slotting in of coins, quarters tumbling down in a jig, sly. Money is deep as skin, knows no enemies like water. Watch me love you a lungful, coming through.

Somewhere near here a young man was killed, picked in a bar and nailed to a fence. Beat all night like a tattered flag, kept the crows away. He too remained resolute on the stakes of the law.

I was not one among that number who called the king wacko, but in that matter too I harbor my shame. Once in a while I doubted his marbles. What with the blanket and naming, what with all that and the other.

I am still wondering about being black enough. The way light sisters wonder if sunscreen remains appropriate for black girls in summer.

And if at all collard greens remain self-affirming.

I am in want of my egg over easy, my sunny-side up. I am still searching for a room dark enough to hang my skin in, let the light come in.

Diallo

I

This was before the sound of the crow, before Cato had confessed
that his life had come to nothing, because the man who ran in his blood,
buried an ocean away, had disowned him for loving a white woman.
Faith, like all stubborn things, lies in things seen. This was before
the color had drained from his American dream.

II

At the trial, friends and family of the officers will sit on one side
of the courtroom, Diallo's parents and supporters on the other,
a scarf of blood between them, spelling the names inscribed
on our crucifix of skin. This is an old tale,
for motion there must be light, for light, shadow.

III

I am not above speaking of trees. Because I am not above speaking
of trees, I will make no condemnation of the forest. I am setting
out to tell you a simple tale, the one with the sound
of Cato hoisting mattresses up the staircase to his American dream,
the wood beneath his boots mournful, as though it knew
the stars in our return. I want to be someone, Cato said, almost with belief.

IV

Here is a scene, Diallo studying by night, his stoic hopes
in a mound beside him, noosed by the chains that sunk
the names of his ancestors in the crossing. Because I am
sentimental he will study by candlelight. Because reason
will prevail, he will study the wisdom of the crow.
This of course is a lie.

V

Because I am intemperate I must infuse the stage with scent.
The scent of burning pines and burning dreams, burning crosses
whose flames have failed to besiege all our history. This will be overkill,
the melodrama of it virtually reducing the facts of the tale to ash.
Because history is the mother of the mob beneath the tree,
I must cloak my precise intentions with care.

VI

There is nothing special about love, Cato said. We were on a stoop
watching the deserted street concede all the day's solid bounty
to mist. We were too hungered by fear, too afraid to find food
in the midnight stretch between here and Africa, as though this too
was not taking our lives into our own hands. When I go back
to Africa, Cato began, before my mind wandered.

VII

I could tell you of the sadness of my father, how like his father
before him he too came from nowhere, a place behind the mountains
two days from the river to the east, how he spent half his life combing
for the names inscribed in his blood. Believing himself defeated,
he spent the latter half conceding all territories of the goodness within him.

VIII

I will make no mention of the weighted chains
quartered in the rage of his dreams, how
even with warmth skin remains unimpeachable.
I must instead restore him to his dream, the one
batting between his eyelids when the first shot comes in.

IX

This happened in a forest. Since I speak of trees

I want to speak of the tree Lumumba must have leaned
against as he faced the firing squad. In his hands
was the corrupt banner of Pan Africanism. Hold still,
said the tree, I will remember.
Lumumba did not know the tree was corrupt.

X

Back then Cato and I spoke of going back home to Africa
as though it was a continent in a dirty suit posing on stilts
in a wax museum. All our goats and the history of their nomenclature
were beside it, the names of good women we wished into marriage.
This would be after our dreams had festered into money.
I want to be someone, Cato said, his voice wrung with longing.

XI

We spoke between salve and skin, between the hours
between shifts, my thumbs kneading the weights
out of the wounds beneath his skin. I want to go
to college, he said, almost with belief.

XII

I am lodged still in the bullet that strikes Amadou's right shin,
the one that burns through bright as a black hole,
and according to the pathologist, travels strikingly upward
until lodged behind the knee. Question of Fact:
at what speed must the flesh receive light to afford it refraction?

XIII

I could tell you about the woman I loved. I could tell you
about the darkness of her silences afterward,
how the light tugged at her slip after she had made love
to another man. I could call this light and shadow.

XIV

Take again the case of the tree with the callused boughs;
the rope and its iron will, stating their claim into the meat of things.
Take afterward the blood heavy on its leaves, the pool
the officer's knee rests in as his hands clasp the dying man's face.

XV

Like all ghosts, this too will seem to come out of nowhere.
Once Cato awoke in the middle of a cane field. The feathers
in his mouth crow black, spelling all forty-one of his ancestors'
names. I want so much to believe in the goodness of the ape within me,
he said, the highway behind us roaring with the weight
of our American dream.

XVI

Because I sometimes cannot breathe I must
use the hooded logic of prowling through the night streets
searching for air. This would be self-evident were my humanism
less punishing, were you too alarmed each time the crow called.

XVII

I could speak of how at night my father tied a headscarf
around his soaped hair trying to make it softer. He believed
the suds caked beneath it would make his hair more European.
He combed open a parting in his hairline separating light and shadow.

XVIII

I too believe equally in the felicity of love
and of blood, of Cato hauling the furniture of his dreams up
the staircase he believed would lead us back to Africa, back to our
homelands rich with their coffee, each step a half life
sloughing off the stains inked within our blood. Who am I to speak?

XIX

Because I am not always angry, I want to speak to you
about earth and sky, pedestrian things, the morning feel of dark smog
brushing against my skin before the light comes in. I want
to speak to you of Diallo's shy ghost in the seawater in the sink
hauling the bale of Cato's dream back to Africa.

XX

After all, here is what I have, the sound of his boots in the vestibule
shaking off the snow; the thrashing of blackbirds full of goodness.
I want to be someone among the plenty of the world,
among the feathers of things. I want a fate more willing than light.

We Must Return

after Agostinho Neto

I.

After the long hours of our reconciliation and philosophy,
after we had solved the troubled existence of our fine people,

C and I had lugged the manikin down the avenue the darkness
nested on the most. It was the first night the sisters

could sell themselves again without lifting their legs to the cops,
nights after the decades-long season they were picked up and raped

for hours in the basement cells at the police station downtown.
C had licked his wounds the longest, and I was getting tired

of the black fumes perfuming the Afropolitanism with us. C
   had theorized
Africans better hang their dreams on sculpted black clay,

and I had grunted my agreement, feeling sly. The sisters cut
troubled eyes at us like we were the Gestapo. The persuasion

of their thighs refracted its way to our groins. But here was C
   theorizing
we had lugged the manikin for what must have been four decades

of misrule too long. C's veins gleamed in the dark, convinced
by his theorizing, something more than truth was troubling him.

I watched him tongue the blood off his palms
where the barroom's elephant grass had cut the deepest.

Dejected, he said, Mulemba could have been his clan name.
It had something to do with his mother.

It was this that cut him to the core. I listened out
for the ape inside me as our voices began climbing over each other

like warring traditions. There was nothing
for me to do, to succumb spelled the funhouse again. I tried not
    to listen

to the honest drag of leg irons shackling C's dreams, their rhythms
sincere and alive like the bonfires the sisters were nursing warming
    the first night.

2.

I was itching to say, Africans had no business with the sea. We
were on First, watching the police put out the lights in an African
    who must

have abominably believed the snake god in the Zambezi River
    would return
clad in the black liberation flag fashioned into an agbada, much to

our chagrin. We stood by and watched, our
heads cool, standard with Hararean apathy, limbs stiff as lands

crowded with crop ghosts and sunshine. I could see the red
tide of his anger begin to breach his blood. With

time, C said, that itch in him could bore its way through you the
    way coffee
with time leaches into the enamel of your teeth. I wanted to be white

the way iron is when troubled most by the fire. With
or without irony. I thought a ball of red cotton

drained out of his mouth, turning my saliva green,
catching the bile, rising. What was it with

African liberators, I wondered, and their need to shuck us down like
    husks off a cob of maize.

The Last Time I Saw Annamore Tsonga

The last time I saw Annamore Tsonga was at the protest in Highfield, the one where people got beaten up and tear-gassed and Gift got shot by the police and later died from excessive blood loss and gunshot wounds. The last time I saw Annamore she was a pile beneath heavy baton sticks and big shiny black boots that branded her body with a swathe of vulgar bruises. It was a Sunday, in Highfield, the last time I saw Annamore Tsonga. It was a prayer meeting. Her lips were heavy with curdled blood. She could barely walk and her face was fat with wounds that suffocated the warm charm of her cheekbones. Later, I could not find her face in the morgue, days after Gift Tandare's funeral, where the police took Gift's body away because too many people wanted to bury him and weep for Zimbabwe. Something about it all reminded me of those scenes on television about apartheid South Africa; mothers crying after their shot babies, bludgeoned sons in police cage-trucks, bludgeoned daughters in blood. How far we thought then, we were from it all.

Preamble to Fever

I will speak briefly before this bread is broken.

Before the matter that occurred regarding him, my brother suffered a myriad of symptoms that refused cohesion. That which took up within him could not be named. Medicine men and women, diviners of all sorts and agendas, did what they could, but their efforts could not carry him. And because it could not be named, the fatigue of it fell upon us. I cannot say all our efforts were futile, but their results I cannot vouch for. Naturally things cannot be said to have become better. Before the matter that occurred regarding him, loud fevers seemed to seize him. They carried him into a stupor in which he seemed to set into words what he witnessed when the fevers climbed higher within him. I have included a few of them here in an effort you make what you can toward a clarity regarding him, regarding the matter that occurred with him later. I could not abandon him; he was my brother.

The Cunning

It came in the days when our money grew on trees. But when it floated down, it lacked the grace of leaves. No one dared pick it. There was the promise of diesel from a rock, the medicine woman had said. And we were thirsty. An orphan girl stood in the red dust and stared. Her begging cup in one hand, an index finger and another stuck beneath her tongue. She had her reservations.

It Came to Pass

Midday Saturday they flocked up the knoll, their staffs in hand. We lit a jealous rumor and warmed our palms over it. We thought them a squad of blind men; the cunning flame would engulf them. It was not a large crowd, the bitter cold not extreme. On the rock, the gray heads cramped together and removed their shoes in reverence. The medicine woman shook. This one would save us, the flesh of our ribs. We watched her lungs levitate, her tongue flail about loosely, troubled by its dreams. She turned the whites of her eyes and summoned for a goat, a bone-white chicken. Then she summoned a bull and they brought her a paddock full of cattle. How distant the spectacle seemed, when she raised her hands to pray. We had missed again the bellied truth in the orphan girl's yellow eyes.

A Town on the Frontier

He was a thin man, shirtless, and in the thick crowd indistinct. He said he carried death in his pouch. His words summoned no crowds among us; he, too, was white-lipped. Like all in our town, he marched on the third day of each month to the blood bank to sell his blood. For hours in the bank he sat still as they drained, his eyes lolling in their sockets. The anxiety wound the nurses tight and sent them into delirium. Wide eyed as beasts, they wailed wall to wall, slamming hard against the concrete till it gave them vertigo. And when they collapsed, they collapsed mechanically onto the floor. They lay still for days, their arms tight around their bellies, spew crusting on their lips. It was the thickening stench that sent him into a frenzy. Liars, he shot out, fanning a fly whisk. Liars, he said, walking about, his ribs clean and clear and tight as dusk's trees. We waited our turn.

Feasts for the Blind

That year it rained crows. Birds fell out of the sky in midflight. Their squawking made mother nervous. It gave her the chills and made her teeth chatter. She threw her eyes everywhere and through the window caught the taut sky tightening. It had been dark for days. I watched her avidly and stabbed her with eyes full of questions. Don't be an idiot, she shot back, the earth too remains hungry. She was going blind, and her mind was beginning to sag. She walked into things and smiled with suffering. She stared into dark corners and hummed into them. She gathered nothing of the swelling whiff but stood by the window and stared hard outside. The beauty of the birds tormented her. In the yellow moonlight they glowed with the threat of better things to come. I licked my lips and heard her mumble inaudibles. She kept her gaze outside, watching the birds fatten, a sour breath gathering among them, a harvest of pus waiting in the wound.

Farther Inland

When she rose again, you lay stomach down on the bed and had her burn a boil out of your behind. You picked the scabs raw to find bitter consolation. Here her fresh fingers, here a fresh tongue. At night on the stoop you listened for crickets. At night the frogs croaked shallow lunged across the ghetto. It was a town full of shadows. You swore to a first confidant in a scuttled hush. You said, Out of the night sky stars tumbled with the velocity of hail, the deception of flitting bats. The house stared into the marsh. The fields were thick with bounty, and she and you, you walked with the confidence of things yet unseen.

Far Country

Later your body would summon boils to itself. Flecks of sunshine nibbled on your skin with the hunger of a locust swarm. The fields were thick with bounty. The house stared into the marsh. On her deathbed she apologized for having you live in the ghetto. For days you watched her die; for days longer you watched as the dust infested her eyes. Outside the ghetto trudged on, the beggar child sang her humble song, pitiful coins clanging into her tin cup, with the loudness of the streets, the thick wagging of tongues, the clamor of steel rods on rusted bicycle rims.

My Dear Menshevik

We found, for months afterward, bright and brilliant corpses bloated on the roadsides. The rains had been heavy, the preceding winds unkind. Squads of famished children marauded the night door to door, searching for food, plucking away women. *Why did the tide of our times turn against us, why did we doubt the flood in the beggar's eyes?* Later we lay for months beneath the shallow moonlight, the field vast and alive with barb-wired specifics—genitals and gauged eyes, purpled buttocks and limbs. It was by their genitals that men had been dragged, mothers hot-waxed. It was you who seized by the clasp the whiff of burning hair riding on the breeze.

As a Moonflower Curious of the Night

Yet again we had doubted the flood in the beggar child's eyes. Her cup no longer clanged. She sat by the roadside and watched, sucking on her fingers. Squads of famished children marauded the night door to door, searching for food. They shouted obscenities and dragged frail men by their belts, plucked away virgins. Months afterward and the bodies would not seize. Mangled corpses churned out of the veld and onto the roadside, bright and shiny and bloated with hot air. She sat by and watched, shaking her head. She was not frantic. She had no part in it. She chewed on nothing but our anguish.

A Hunger

We had tried everything before we took up arms. Our clothing had flayed off our skins and through what remained for tatters our mangled bodies shone. Fat men ballooned with the hunger and bit off their nails to feed their offspring. They sniffed at everything for food. And because they sniffed they began to grunt and from this they grew snouts like red river hogs. We feared our scent on the wind would betray us. There was a prized harvest of the dry skin that peeled off our scabs. We saved it for currency. We moved in the night with the wind on our side. We clawed for roots and tubers but away from the river. There were those that had warned us matters would come to such. Soon we hoped we would empty out of the city, and on its borders, again, our bodies would glow.

The City

We did with the city what we could. We fanned the fumes from its ruins and observed them carefully, eager to divine its secrets. It was not all smoke. Colonies stitched their way across the banks of the river, their vibrancy palpable. We stared out at them and nodded to ourselves, applauding our efforts. We trudged about and salvaged the remains of past civilizations. Stretches of asphalt that betrayed old roads. Shards of cheap crockery and half-burnt books, dolls with singed hair. Fat men loitered in abandoned alleyways. They clasped their offspring to their chests like secrets. They cast telling eyes on us. Out in the distance, the begging cup still clanged.

////

Preamble to In the Case Regarding My Brother

Of this I needed no proof. My brother was the ape inside me, I could tell. It had taken him years to gestate. He turned and turned within me with all the will of vertigo. I could tell the eye of his gusts, but I stood tall. My brother took root.

He had no date set for his birth, and he set none—not that I can recall. My brother grew slowly within me like a root. I lugged to him all my doubts and nursed him. What else could I do, everything knew its way around everything else. But he spared me no effort. He was my brother.

Requiem: In the Case Regarding My Brother

I

Through me ran the river. Through me ran the river hollowed out
by goodness, a thicket of skulls, jaws intact, the countenance in their
faces still grimacing the face of death.

Halos quivered feverishly above the black waters, waiting.

I mentioned nothing of the exertions between my brother and me,
our losses stood prodigal.

11

My brother blamed everything on everything else. Wounded by goodness he kept now only the counsel of himself.

Unable to hear him, I said, sounding like a nut, Being is becoming.

I could not dismiss him.

He believed there was more to facts than pedestrian somnambulism. But I could hear only the thrashing of hail on the face of the river. I could hear the sound gather within my brother and consume him.

III

Once I caught a bough leaping into the air, a thicket of birds lifting off of it, dissolving among the stars.

Bridgehead, mast, a lungful of god.

I watched my brother wade deeper into the waters, his shoulders arched like a bow.

IV

Because the river ran through me, I was flooded with its longing. I wanted near me only blood, I said.

I wanted near me only blood that had known the wrath of empire.

But all I could hear was the wrath of black hail beating through my brother. I stilled myself and listened.

v

My brother contended all waves carried tension.

Alone at night he heard our skinfolk tug out of the water. The hymns in their feet, he said, carried no sheet music.

Wing after wing lifting from each bough.

VI

Beyond the banks of the river lay the tortured mountains.

Because the mountains were stoic, I could not bruise them with bitterness.

Because the heavens were named in darkness, I could not claim them as my own.

VII

My brother said something was tightening within him. He was look-
ing, he said, for more space to move within his skin.

I worried with understanding. It was a hunger I knew could not be
diminished. Colossal in its cravings, unimpeachable with its facts.

The sculpture he was building fashioned a cage around him. On its roof,
drawn out bales of cotton, a thicket of nooses dangling like neckties.

The leg irons, he said, were the only symbolism.

VIII

Because belief too is an act of faith, I believed the wound in my brother would liberate him to the music within him.

Standing together I believed I could feel the seams where within him earth met sky, where the blood in our marrow revealed the horned truth of our conception.

But my brother heaved full of pleading; everything was taut within him, the torment busy, arching his shoulders.

I waited for him farther along; he was my brother.

IX

I want to forgive you for not knowing what I am speaking of.

Once, in a single seating, I watched him with his bare hands fashion a chisel out of a rock.

Against his chest, the thrashing of birds lifting from the boughs within him, the chaos that hung in the air like a cape before their squawking began.

X

There was no harm in my brother. He stood for what he stood; did what before him waited to be done. I believe his beliefs lacked the extravagance of his faith. The beams above his head, lean long torsos, bough upon bough full of harmonious song.

Because the mountains were stoic, I could not bruise them with bitterness.

Because the heavens were named with darkness, I could not claim them as my own.

Oak, pine, chestnut, and song.

I could hear the muted songs balled like fists in the chests of the mountains.

I watched my brother wade deeper into the waters, the skulls bobbing on either side of him. The slick light made my brother glow, the hailstones about him shining quietly, melting into the moonlight.

XII

We laid out the yokes alongside each other on the banks of the river.

I want to believe I must have made a remark about nothing trivial, but the lugging would not tire him, the river would not concede.

XIII

I want to say I was filled only with the longings of the river. But I could not resist that which had claimed me. I had been named by their patience.

I would like to say I abhorred their invitations; that I found little to no appeal in their seductions.

The beams above his head resembled the frustrated arms of scarecrows. I turned pleadingly to my brother, but all I could muster was the blood beating into my mouth.

XIV

Unable to locate a fragrance, he rubbed dry sage to a fish head and carved a window into a wall. He believed if it faced the forest we could gather with our eyes what the forest remembered.

I could not disprove him. He believed warmth was a creed all living things abided by.

The hunger within him worried me with song.

XV

After the long hours he said, The night remained unrepentant. Then
he dragged all the yokes back to the waters and laid them in a coffle.

Each skull remembered its name, the patient weight of its yoke.

Because the river remembered, my brother would not forget.

XVI

Once, in the moonlight, I caught a noose in the river melting into a halo.

Wise caller, maladies serene in the morning light.

The beams he dealt with remembered pale skin and bruises.

He understood only that which was before him, what the moon could name of itself between clouds, the song in the morning dew. Because the river remembered, my brother would not forget.

XVII

A creed he lived by: nothing with horns could be wrapped for too long.

Two things he knew of the heavens:

1) No light so assertive could reveal them with honesty.

2) That which we all knew of the heavens, which cannot be unnamed.

XVIII

I want to forgive you for not knowing what I am speaking of.

I want to forgive you for the free song my brother strangled in the cave of his mouth. I want to forgive you for the song my brother strangled inside of him after his exertions.

I cannot say with confidence that my brother lacked belief. I cannot attest that in the end, he was without bitterness. Like all things good my brother's song underlined only preambles.

XIX

I wanted so much to believe there was more to everything than the embers of things. I wanted to believe only music could name the honest symbolism regarding my brother. There was nothing sinister in him.

Wise caller, bridgehead, anchor full of dust.

XX

My brother contended all waves carried tension. Against every beach he contended he heard footsteps hulk out of the waters. There was nothing sinister about it, he said, no one was skulking.

In the end there was nothing left of my brother after his exertions. But what is good is good. In his sleep my brother let the choruses lift out of him, they seeped out of his mouth through a crook of his lips.

I cocked my ears and listened.

He said nothing of his illuminations. I could not dismiss him. He was my brother.

Mugarandega

1. NATSA KWAUNOBVA KWAUNOENDA HUSIKU

Alone, in a foreign land, she picked out each morning avocados to shampoo her hair. Only the ripe ones, like luck knew when to exercise their grace, the ground beneath them sleeved moist with dew. Luck, she said, was all eyes and patient quivering. Wounded with strangeness, she married a man with sweet flora for a tongue. His height, she believed, revealed the aloe in him, his furrowed clouds the rage of flame lilies. The year of the Federation of Nyasaland and Rhodesia, she said, bad mushroom had saved us from the Portuguese, the mosquito Dahomey. Still, in the wet season, I dream of the soft pit in her flesh, the quiver of her hand in the dew.

*

2. MANAKIRA KURE MVURA YEMUBVUMBI

We sat in the night under the trees watching the river and its fortitude, drawn out and taut, anxious as catapults. When an arrow desires it most, it leaps alone off the bow to find the flesh on its own. In the dark, his body quivered magical with nerves, the spell of the river fetching him. In my mouth, beneath my tongue, the unnamed pits of my fears. The water, we knew, fed its own beasts. Across it, he said, spread the rest of our lives—the plush dreams we had offered the women we were to marry, the soft cheeks of our future children fat with good health, shade we were to scurry beneath. In my blood beat the woman who fashioned a soup from boiling stones. In my blood beat the woman wounded with strangeness. When an arrow desires flesh most, it leaps alone off the bow. Night sky ricocheting off the water. In their eyes the beasts carried loud stars and satellites, the hollow seat of the chariot in the moon's blind eye awaiting us on the other side.

3. AKANGA NYIMO AVANGARARA

You never know when something truly begins. Where the men ponder a fire on a winter's night, a boy carries a pouch, rises to be a satellite elsewhere. Still after all these years, you remain attracted to graveyards. The sight of tombstones stitching their way across the train's passing window quilts you in silence. Once, in a foreign land, you muttered confusedly, *Breath is a syllable cremation cannot afford*, then alighted the train to hug the first African you saw, because they were African. The scent of his sweat, raw shea butter, sage, and cinnamon. His glow carried you back up the mountains. Flame lilies and lavender, aloe and rose. Still after all you wish to be buried among your kin. You fear the weight of return the way you fear in death the earth pressing down against your corpse will snap your clavicle into two. It will be a fiasco among the sleeping dead, the commotion lateral and carrying on for days. With neither wife nor a child, they will bury you with a mouse. Remember still, dear stranger, stranger shores before you breached more reluctant waters, the ground beneath them pitted, still moist with the dew.

*

In the Throat of the Heaven's Guide

And should the revolution take place between your thighs, brother leader, blame hallucinogenics; it is only the mothers of the brave who weep, and my blood is weak with forgetting; how it trembles.

They will peel him out of a hole like Hussein. Or a mansion in Abbottabad. There is air and non-air. My friend tells me the colonel prefers tents, and face cream, things with meaning.

Perhaps they will find him in a French boutique in Tunis, lipsticked and getting his hair done like the sisters up in Harlem, air conditioning across summer.

Still, mother, I do not believe in the music of oceans; too many of my bones want to return home. The beating of my blood, Angola.

And should the revolution take place between your thighs, brother leader, pick the itch: there is no honor in clenched teeth. There is air and non-air.

My friend tells me that after the urethra's slow hymn and the gunmetal blues of other genitalia, eventually the syphilis climbs upriver to claim the mind. Still there is no truer love.

What blues jig seizes these feet; what wailing in flight like glorious comets.

And should the revolution take place between your thighs, brother leader, execute a strategic retreat. What saves us but the wind through the eye. Burn, Bab al-Azizia, burn.

He will be in his desert library taking a nap in a womb chair between Nietzsche and Gogol, eyes behind shades. There is air and non-air.

My friend tells me he has a sweet tooth for agbada and Gabbana. They will find him in a mall flowing in the rivers of his robes. He will want penicillin and a pack of Doritos.

Still, I often wonder about Sani Abacha, the Viagra, and whether the Indian women knew of Mobutu and the hemorrhoid; the scent of hours the sheik burnt watching himself, pitch-perfecting.

Always I am a slave, half-ape, half-child. What saves us but the wind through the eye.

Born of the gun. Give me sight, so I too may see. An eye for an eye, our scrambled world.

ACKNOWLEDGMENTS

The following poems have previously appeared in the following publications:

Cincinnati Review: "The City," "As a Moonflower Curious of the Night"

Copper Nickel: "In the Throat of the Heaven's Guide," "You Don't Want the Light to Find Out What You've Done," "Catechism"

The Journal: "It Came to Pass," "Farther Inland"

Laurel Review: "A Town on the Frontier," "The Cunning"

Pleiades: "A Hunger," "Far Country"

Plume: "My Dear Menshevik," "Feasts for the Blind"

Prairie Schooner: "In the Name of the Tongue," "The Last Time I Saw Annamore Tsonga"

I want to thank the editors and staff of these publications for their generosity.

"Diallo" is informed by the shooting of Amadou Diallo, an African immigrant from Guinea, West Africa, shot and killed by four NYPD officers in New York City, February 4, 1999. The first two lines in part ii are taken directly from an article published in the *New York Times* during the trial.

In "Ota Benga Returns to the Congo," the lines "the secretary of the zoo at the time . . . Caucasians" are taken from rt.com, which carries an article on this case. The words of Reverend James H. Gordon ("Our race, we think, / is depressed enough without exhibiting / one of us with the apes") are directly quoted from the *New York Times*, September 11, 1906. "Every wanderer feels a little tickling in his heels," "The first thing I learned was to shake hands," and "My report will not teach the Academy anything basically new" are from "A Report to the Academy" by Franz Kafka.

"In the Throat of the Heaven's Guide" alludes to and employs refrains that echo both Gil Scott-Heron's and Sarah Jones's works, "The Revolution Will Not Be Televised" and "Your Revolution" respectively.

MUGARANDEGA

Mugarandega loosely translates to mean a "loneliness borne out of migration." Each of the parts in this poem is opened by a Shona proverb. *Natsa kwaunobva kwaunoenda husiku* loosely translates as "leave your place of departure in good books as you do not know how you will be received where you are going." *Manakira kure mvura yemubvumbi* loosely translates to "things only look good from a distance"; *Akanga nyimo avangarara* loosely means "them who have chosen to roast round nuts must stay the course."

To order or obtain more information on these or other University of Nebraska Press titles, visit nebraskapress.unl.edu. For more information about the African Poetry Book Series, visit africanpoetrybf.unl.edu.

CPSIA information can be obtained
at www.ICGtesting.com
Printed in the USA
LVHW02s2312230118
563703LV00004B/354/P